GARDEN GUIDES

ROSES

GARDEN GUIDES

ROSES

LINDSAY BOUSFIELD

Illustrations by
ELAINE FRANKS

A Siena book.
Siena is an imprint of Parragon Books.

This edition first published in 1996 by
Parragon Book Service Ltd
Unit 13–17, Avonbridge Trading Estate
Atlantic Road
Avonmouth
Bristol BS11 9QD

Produced by
Robert Ditchfield Ltd
Combe Court
Kerry's Gate
Hereford HR2 0AH

ISBN 0 75251 625 6

A copy of the British Library Cataloguing in Publication Data is
available from the Library.

Typeset by Action Typesetting Ltd, Gloucester
Colour origination by Mandarin Offset Ltd, Hong Kong
Printed and bound in Italy

ACKNOWLEDGEMENTS

Most of the photographs were taken in the author's nursery, Acton Beauchamp Roses, Worcester. The publishers
would also like to thank the many people and organizations who have allowed photographs to be taken for this
book, including the following:

Lallie Cox, Woodpeckers, Bidford-on-Avon; Dinmore Manor; Richard Edwards, Well Cottage, Blakemere; Lance
Hattatt, Arrow Cottage, Weobley; Mottisfont Rose Garden (National Trust); Mr and Mrs R. Norman, Marley Bank,
Whitbourne; Pentwyn Cottage Garden, Bacton; Powis Castle (National Trust); RHS Garden, Wisley; Mary Ann
Robinson; Raymond Treasure, Stockton Bury Farm, Kimbolton; Mr and Mrs S de R Wall; Wyevale Garden Centre,
Hereford.

Photographs of the following roses are reproduced by kind permission of Mattocks Roses (Notcutts, Woodbridge,
Suffolk): 'City Lights', 'Perestroika', 'Queen Mother', 'Regensburg', 'Royal William', 'Scarlet Patio', 'Simba', 'Valois
Rose'.

Photographs of the following roses are reproduced by kind permission of the author: Compassion, Hermosa,
Irene Watts, Leverkusen, Perle d'Or, Sombreuil.

CONTENTS

POISONOUS PLANTS

In recent years, concern has been voiced about poisonous plants or plants which can cause allergic reactions if touched. The fact is that many plants are poisonous, some in a particular part, others in all their parts. For the sake of safety, it is always, without exception, essential to assume that no part of a plant should be eaten unless it is known, without any doubt whatsoever, that the plant or its part is edible and that it cannot provoke an allergic reaction in the individual person who samples it. It must also be remembered that some plants can cause severe dermatitis, blistering or an allergic reaction if touched, in some individuals and not in others. It is the responsibility of the individual to take all the above into account.

How to Use This Book

Where appropriate, approximate measurements of a plant's height have been given, and also the spread where this is significant, in both metric and imperial measures. The height is the first measurement, as for example 1.2m × 60cm/4 × 2ft. However, both height and spread vary so greatly from garden to garden since they depend on soil, climate and position, that these measurements are offered as guides only. This is especially true of trees and shrubs where ultimate growth can be unpredictable.

The following symbols are also used throughout the book:

    ○ = thrives best or only in full sun
    ◑ = thrives best or only in part-shade
    ● = succeeds in full shade
    E = evergreen

Where no sun symbol and no reference to sun or shade is made in the text, it can be assumed that the plant tolerates sun or light shade.

Plant Names

For ease of reference this book gives the botanical name under which a plant is most widely listed for the gardener. These names are sometimes changed and in such cases the new name has been included. Common names are given wherever they are in frequent use.

ROSES

THE ROSE FAMILY, or *Rosa*, which is Latin for 'rose', has captured imaginations for thousands of years with its myths, legends and symbolism. Steeped in history, the rose embraces a kaleidoscope of tones in numerous exquisite flower shapes; its prickles and foliage parade a diverse range of habits unrivalled by any other plant family. Roses are classified according to these distinguishing characteristics, beginning with Wild roses and developing through history as man took up rose cultivation.

Species roses or Wild roses are native to many regions of the northern hemisphere. Their unique and distinctive features grace any place, yielding year round interest: Wild yellow roses boast elegance of habit; Sweetbriars exude richly aromatic foliage; Cinnamon roses and unusual species fascinate with peeling stems, winged thorns and bristly shoots; Dog roses charm with their simple flowers; Rugosas flaunt their ornamental hips.

Old Shrub roses are natural hybrids of Species roses. Rose breeding got under way when man collected and cultivated them. By the end of the eighteenth century Albas, Gallicas, Damasks and Moschatas prevailed, culminating in the development of Centifolias and Moss roses. Their balance of foliage and flowers is perfect and their fragrance and flower-shapes are unrivalled.

Western rose culture was revolutionized when breeders began crossing *Rosa chinensis* hybrids, introduced from the east, with Old Shrub roses. A new race of roses was born: the Autumn Damasks (Portland roses), Bourbons and Hybrid Perpetuals, which inherited the Old rose fragrance and flower-shapes, but yielded the ability to repeat-flower – virtually unknown at the time. Their distinctive appearance and flexibility of habit inspired innovative design for new rose gardens.

(*Left*) A good combination: *Viola cornuta alba* twines comfortably through the branches of an old moss rose. Violas thrive better if they are planted on the shady side of roses.

(*Right*) Spreading bushes of Gallica roses: the pink 'Président de Sèze' and the crimson 'Charles de Mills' notable for the quartered 'sliced off' formation of its flowers. Both roses are very scented but only once-flowering.

Modern Shrub roses are relatively recent introductions and include: Hybrid Species roses, closely related to the Species roses; famous old favourites like the Dwarf Polyanthas (Poly-Poms); the outstandingly floriferous Hybrid Musks; and recent hybrid groups such as English roses and Ground-cover roses.

Large-flowered Climbers are often climbing versions or 'sports' from a shrub or bush rose. Climbing Noisettes bear clusters of small, sweetly fragrant flowers in soft hues. Ramblers are in three groups (all fragrant) distinguished by their ancestry: Sempervirens Ramblers bear exquisite clusters of small flowers; Multiflora Ramblers have upright growth and large trusses of small flowers; and Wichuraiana Ramblers produce elegant sprays of rather larger flowers.

Modern Bush roses are the most popular roses of the twentieth century: they differ from Shrub roses in being generally short and compact, and dominated by the flowers which they bear. Vividness and brightness are key characteristics. Although many alluring hues may be found among the Floribundas (Cluster-flowered roses), and multicoloured and hand-painted effects among the Miniature and Patio roses, it is the Hybrid Teas that embody the history of man's pursuit of the perfect bloom.

Standard roses come in miniature, half and full-standard stems. Depending on the type of rose budded onto the stem, it produces a ball, mop-head or weeping-standard. Standard roses are most useful in formal gardens where they add dimension and may be used to 'float the eye' across massed plantings.

The Dwarf Polyantha (or Poly-Pom) rose, 'Francine Austin', grown as a standard.

SITING

When choosing roses the site should be the principal consideration. There are certain conditions which roses will not tolerate: dense shade, waterlogged ground, poor soil, soil which has a high lime content, and soil which has already been growing roses.

An exposed site is best suited to Rugosas or Scotch briars, whereas Dwarf Polyanthas (Poly-Poms), China roses and English roses need enclosure and protection. Dog roses, Wild Yellow roses, Sweetbriars, Cinnamon roses and Albas mostly tolerate semi-shade, suiting woodland plantings as well as wild gardens, where Ramblers can soar up into trees or smother secret arbours. Large, open or moderately exposed spaces can be broken up with informal groups of giant Hybrid Species roses, while carpets and cascades of Ground-cover roses can colour the vista. Damasks, Centifolias and Hybrid Musks make excellent floriferous, fragrant screens and hedges to protect the mixed borders of the inner garden, which must abound with Gallicas, Moss Roses, Autumn Damasks, Bourbons and Hybrid Perpetuals. Arches and pergolas used to line walkways create controlled vistas festooned with Climbing Noisettes and Ramblers. Large-flowered Climbers are best suited to wall and trellis.

It would be true to say Hybrid Teas and Floribundas look out of place among Old Shrub roses – better in a bed of their own. Although many smaller Old Shrub roses do grow successfully in pots – they should not be positioned beside Miniatures in a tiny patio or courtyard!

PROPAGATION AND TIMING

Traditionally roses were 'budded' in the field onto 'rootstocks' and lifted in autumn, after they had been hardened-off by frost, to be sold bare-rooted while they were still in their dormant state. They were thus planted in autumn – before nurserymen put them in containers for sale all year round. Keen gardeners always rushed to plant then, to catch the warmth in the soil and get them going before atrocious winters set in. Very sensible! Their roses had all winter and spring to get watered-in and properly established ready for a magnificent show in summer.

The advent of container roses has encouraged wider use of 'cuttings', which has the advantage of no 'suckers' (see below) – attractive particularly to the large scale landscaper. 'Bench-grafting' under glass hastens the production line for commercial breeders as well as making propagation of non-hardy varieties possible.

Some varieties of roses lend themselves to 'layering' (pinning a stem in the soil to form roots and thus a new plant) and 'division' as successful self-propagating methods. Only first generation Species roses will come true from seed.

PLANTING

Apart from considerations of the height and spread of a rose, spacing is a matter of design: 'How dense do you want them?'

Planting An Individual Rose Have to hand a barrow of 'organic matter' comprised of well-rotted horse manure, mixed with peat or cocoa-fibre and three handfuls of bonemeal

'Cornelia' is one of the best of the scented and long-flowering hybrid musk roses. The white St Bernard's lily (*Anthericum liliago*) grows in front, enjoying the same conditions, sun and well-drained soil, as the rose.

or the like. Prepare a hole at least 60cm/2ft diameter by digging out the topsoil to a depth of about 23cm/9in and put it to one side – use a polythene sheet. Break up 23cm/9in subsoil in the bottom of the hole, and discard about half, replacing with and incorporating organic matter. Put some of the topsoil back into the hole working in more organic matter to a nice friable mixture forming a mound in the centre. Place the plant into the hole, spreading the roots out over the

(Left) The wonderful once-flowering modern rose 'Constance Spry', which has the rare scent of myrrh. Normally grown as a lax shrub, its display is even more sumptuous here as a climber trained on a wall.

(Right) A mixed bed of shrub roses and foxgloves: the crimson 'Gipsy Boy', the pink Centifolia rose 'De Meaux' and the small perennial foxglove, *Digitalis lutea*.

mound (or carefully remove the container) so that the 'union' (where the shoots and roots join) is 2.5cm/1in–5cm/2in below the ground level – allowing for settlement. Work the rest of the topsoil and organic matter back into the hole round the roots, firming well as you go. Water well and mulch, to preserve moisture and keep the soil active. Roses planted during spring and summer should be kept watered until established.

Planting A Bed of Roses The soil preparation itself is best done in advance, i.e. 'double-digging' or digging to two spade depths. Don't discard any subsoil as this is unnecessary unless finished levels are crucial.

Pests and Diseases It is true some roses are less prone to diseases than others but including them in a routine spraying programme will do no harm. Rust, blackspot and mildew pose the greatest threats and as in most things prevention is better than cure. During the dormant season apply tar-wash (Phenol), and as soon as the leaves emerge commence two-weekly applications of fungicide (Myclobutanil) for the first half of summer (then change it). Pay particular attention to the undersides of leaves. Treat harmful blackfly with pesticide (Primicarb) which may be combined with most fungicides. It is also worthwhile including concentrated seaweed extract.

been grafted or 'budded'. The consequence is sapping of the strength of the rose and ultimately takeover or 'reversion'. Suckers are easily recognizable by their vigorous erect stems, and Dog rose type flowers and foliage. They grow from below the graft or union, from whence they should be removed. To cut them off won't suffice – they'll thrive on the experience. Rather, they must be torn off at the point where they shoot from the rootstock.

PRUNING

Principles Rose pruning on anything other than Hybrid Teas and Floribundas is a very controversial topic. The prime purpose of it is, and will always be, to stimulate growth, to maintain shape, and to train. It can be carried out in summer after flowering, as well as in winter. Pruning removes twiggy, old or dead branches and shortens others. It can be executed radically or with minute precision (never mind the principles!) according to the personality of the gardener.

Pruning Methods To trim and shape, reduce canes or amputate the previous season's growth, make a cut angled away from a bud. Use sharp secateurs. To remove old or dead branches, make an angled cut down to the base. Use a pruning saw.

For mass amputation, use a hedge-trimmer or shears.

Hand-cuts should always be clean. Ragged and torn edges look atrocious, but a beautifully executed radical pruning operation looks a treat. Mechanical pruning is a godsend, but afterwards take a holiday until the leaves emerge!

Feeding In early spring after pruning, established roses will thank you for a handful of bonemeal or the like raked into the surface of the soil and a thick mulching with well-rotted horse manure. Repeat in midsummer, after dead-heading, particularly on varieties which repeat-flower.

Dead-heading The removal of spent flowers encourages production of new flowering shoots on repeat-flowering roses. Make the cut above the second or third leaf below the truss or flower stem. Leave roses with ornamental hips.

Suckers These are breakthroughs of the parent plant or rootstock onto which a rose has

1. Species Roses (Wild Roses)

*Fine, large, naturally elegant shrubs –
bearing unique and distinctive stems,
thorns, foliage and hips. Their
charming fresh single flowers are
harbingers of the rose season!*

Top down: **'Stanwell Perpetual'** (Scotch briar), *Rosa villosa* **'Duplex'**, **'Mary Queen of Scots'**, and right **'Lady Penzance'** (Sweetbriar). Sweetbriars, Scotch briars and Dog roses tumble together. *Rosa eglanteria* was a favourite in medieval gardens grown alongside Old Shrub roses such as Albas, Gallicas and Damasks.

DOG ROSES (*ROSA CANINA*), WHICH GRACE SUMMER HEDGEROWS with extrovert displays of their numerous variants; Sweetbriars (*Rosa eglanteria*), famous for their apple-scented foliage which fills the air, especially after rain; and Scotch briars (*Rosa pimpinellifolia*), thriving in exposed windy sites, glowing with their bronze-tinted miniature foliage and numerous small, scented, sweet flowers – are all wild roses.

DOG ROSES *and* BRIARS

Rosa complicata (*Rosa canina* × *Rosa gallica* hybrid) Large, flat, single shocking-pink flowers with pale cream eye and golden boss. Good as a hedge. 1.5 × 2m/5 × 6ft

***Rosa canina* 'Andersonii'** Deep, brilliant rose-pink variant of the Dog rose. Light green glaucous stems and tough downy grey-green foliage. Rich raspberry fragrance. 2 × 2.4m/6 × 8ft

Rosa pimpinellifolia (The Scotch Burnett Rose) A low-growing spreading shrub, ideal for ground cover, thriving in poor conditions. Single white flowers borne in profusion. 1 × 1m/3 × 3ft.

WILD YELLOW ROSES

As if contrapuntal to winter's 'yellow flush', the Wild yellow roses hail their unique golden chorus as harbingers of the rose season, triumphant that it is now early summer! The textured stems are in keeping with the diverse habit of each species which typically bears small fern-like foliage, yellow flowers and occasionally hips.

'Cantabrigiensis' ('The Cambridge Rose') Elegant upright habit – bristly brown stems with fern-like foliage turning bronze. Primrose-yellow flowers followed by bright orange-red hips. 2.2 × 2m/7 × 6ft

Rosa hugonis A graceful shrub – almost thornless, bearing tiny fern-like foliage with small, cupped primrose-yellow flowers arranged along its airy, arching, wiry twigs. 2.2 × 2m/7 × 6ft

'Canary Bird' (above and left) Bright canary-yellow single flowers, smooth red-brown stems with soft-green, dainty fern-like foliage. Very early with a second crop in late summer. 2.2 × 2.2m/7 × 7ft

◆ _'Canary Bird' is often grown as a standard rose._

STRIKING FEATURES OTHER THAN FLOWERS, such as stems, thorns and foliage are useful for creating interesting textures and focal points in a mixed border, wild garden and hedge. Aromatic foliage discloses the presence of Cinnamon roses, and the brightness of sumptuous shining ornamental hips ends the rose season with a chorus, as the birds commence their banquet!

Rosa roxburghii ('Chestnut Rose') Large, single pink flowers with white centres and bright golden stamens. 2.2 × 2.2m/7 × 7ft

CINNAMON ROSES *and* UNUSUAL SPECIES

Rosa glauca (*Rosa rubrifolia*) Maroon bloom-covered stems with glaucous foliage. Clusters of small pink flowers with white eye. 2 × 1.2m/6 × 4ft

***Rosa moyesii* 'Geranium'** Glowing single blood-red flowers with golden-yellow stamens, borne along arching upright thorny stems. 2.4 × 2.2m/8 × 7ft

***Rosa californica* 'Plena'** Dark-pink semi-double flowers. 2.4 × 2.1m/8 × 7ft

◆ *This dense upright shrub makes a good specimen planting.*

RUGOSA ROSES

THE WILD ROSES OF JAPAN. Sturdy, stocky bushes with bright green luxuriant foliage with deeply veined leaves and large richly fragrant, tissue-textured flowers in early summer. Huge, round, orangey-red hips often coincide with intermittent mid to late summer crops. Excellent shrubs in the border, as hedging or specimens. They withstand poor soil conditions, exposed sites and are disease resistant.

'Agnes' Large blooms amid quite small, pewter grey-green leaves. Very thorny growth. 1.5 × 1.2m/5 × 4ft

'Fimbriata' ('Phoebe's Frilled Pink') Clusters of small pale pink fimbriated (frilled) flowers with darker pink and white tones. Soft light-green foliage. Few thorns. 1 × 1m/3 × 3ft

Autumn planted bare-root roses establish better with winter's own rain and stand up to late spring frosts. Order early direct from the grower!

'Blanc Double de Coubert' Large, open semi-double, pure-white blooms, of delicate tissue paper texture. 1.5 × 1.2m/5 × 4ft

◆ *This rose is exceptionally fragrant and flowers most of the summer.*

'Fru Dagmar Hastrup' Deep pink buds opening to single rose-pink flowers with conspicuous creamy stamens. 1.2 × 1.2m/4 × 4ft

'Moje Hammarberg' Large, very fragrant flowers produced freely throughout summer. 1.2 × 1m/4 × 3ft

At the back of this planting, **'Sarah van Fleet'**, **'Moje Hammarberg'** and *Salvia nemerosa* 'Superba', and in the foreground **'Fimbriata'** and *Pulmonaria saccharata* 'Alba'. A shapely, apparently deep border/hedge. Contrasting tones, textures and forms keep the eye busy, never fathoming the actual depth of the border.

21

RUGOSA ROSES

'Sarah van Fleet' Clusters of semi-double, cool mallow-pink tinged with lilac, flowers. Richly fragrant and very perpetual. Large luxuriant foliage. Makes a beautiful hedge. Prone to rust. 1.5 × 1m/5 × 3ft

Most Rugosas require little skilful maintenance beyond trimming to shape in winter – as hard as you like to; but trim Grootendorsts very hard.

Planting deeply (so that the 'union' is 2.5cm/1in–5cm/2in below ground level) discourages 'suckers', and prevents 'rocking' on a windy exposed site.

Bountiful hips often coincide with the second and third crops of flowers – be sure not to dead-head these varieties!

'Mrs Anthony Waterer' An arching vigorous bush massed with fragrant semi-double flowers mainly in summer. 1.2 × 1.5m/4 × 5ft

'Pink Grootendorst' Tinted salmon in bud, opening to striking rose-pink, small fimbriated flowers, borne in clusters. 1.2 × 1m/4 × 3ft

***Rosa rugosa* 'Alba'** Large single, silky, pure-white flowers. Blooms intermittently throughout summer. 2 × 2m/6 × 6ft

'Roseraie de l'Haÿ' Beautifully pointed buds opening to richly scented, fully double flowers of rich crimson-purple. Bright healthy foliage and fine autumn colouring. 2 × 1.5m/6 × 5ft

'Scabrosa' A compact leafy shrub bearing very large, single, light crimson-mauve flowers with creamy stamens, followed by enormous orange-red hips. Recurrent flowering. 1.5 × 1.2m/5 × 4ft

As the season of 'mellow fruitfulness' autumn is naturally equipped with dramatic stage sets and lighting for the final dance! Turgid clusters of bright red rose hips will dazzle us against a brilliant blue sky, glow seductively by the low golden-red autumn sunlight which sinks so fast, and twinkle like treasure along boughs laden with snow.

Rosa rugosa **'Alba'**

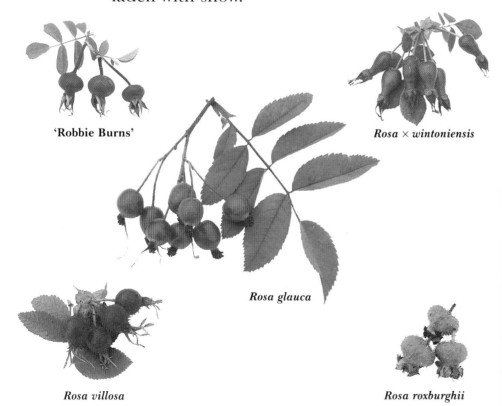

'Robbie Burns'

Rosa × wintoniensis

Rosa glauca

Rosa villosa

Rosa roxburghii

Rosa moyesii

2. Old Shrub Roses (Summer Flowering)

Forerunners as garden shrubs for perfect composition of foliage and flowers; unrivalled among all roses for fragrance and flower shapes.

In the background white foxgloves and angelicas mingle with *Rosa* **'Mundi'** and **'Charles de Mills'**, whilst in the foreground **'Empress Josephine'** sits amongst purple sage and lavender. Versatile Gallicas were traditionally grown alongside herbs in the apothecary's garden.

ROSA GALLICA DATES BACK TO THE TWELFTH CENTURY B.C. to the Medes and Persians, and it was the first rose to be cultivated in the Middle East. The Romans brought it to Europe where it became the principal parent of the Old Shrub roses. Tough spreading shrubs thriving under the poorest conditions but not in shade. Solitary, upheld, very double richly fragrant blooms in exotic hues of crimson purple and maroon.

GALLICA ROSES

'Duc de Guiche' Globular flowers of crimson-magenta with purple veins and stripes – quartered with green eye. Spreading arching branches with dark foliage. 1.2 × 1.2m/4 × 4ft

Rosa 'Mundi' (*Rosa gallica versicolor*) Pale rosy-pink blotched and striped with cerise-pink. Very fragrant. 1.2 × 1.2m/4 × 4ft

◆ *Rosa 'Mundi' is often grown as a hedge.*

'Charles de Mills' The 'sliced off' appearance shows the petals remarkably whorled and quartered. 1.5 × 1.2m/5 × 4ft

It is lore that any shoot bearing seven leaves is a 'sucker'. Most shrub roses have seven leaves. 'Suckers' are normally quite easily distinguishable.

Gallicas often spread themselves monopodially underground – in time, one bush can form into a substantial thicket. These are not 'suckers'.

'Empress Josephine' (*Rosa × francofurtana*) Deeply veined grey-green foliage and smooth stems, bearing rose-pink blooms, veined and flushed with mauve, followed by turbinate hips. 1 × 1.2m/3 × 4ft

Die unto themselves sweet Roses do not so, Of their sweet deaths are the sweetest odours made. (Rosa gallica officinalis) Shakespeare.

GALLICA ROSES

Never replace old rose beds with new roses without excavating and changing 45cm/1½ft depth of soil, or else rest it for three years.

Rosa gallica officinalis
('The Apothecary's Rose', 'Red Rose of Lancaster'). Very fragrant. 1.2 × 1.2m/ 4 × 4ft

'Camaieux' Striking semi-double loosely formed white flowers striped and splashed with crimson and purple. 1.5 × 1m/5 × 3ft

'Tuscany Superb' Large, full, semi-double blooms of intense dark crimson-maroon fading to violet-maroon. 1.5 × 1m/5 × 3ft

'Président de Sèze' ('Jenny Duval') Striking two-toned, fully double blooms, of dark magenta-crimson in the centre, paling to lilac-white round the edges. 1.5m × 90cm/5 × 3ft

◆ *Flowering branches may need staking to support the weight of blooms.*

ROSA DAMASCENA, OFFSPRING OF *ROSA GALLICA* AND *ROSA PHOENICIA*. Introduced from Damascus by the Crusaders, Damasks were cultivated, by the Romans, principally for the production of attar of roses (rose oil). For this they remain famous today. Sturdy shrubs, with bristly, thorny stems and deeply veined, downy grey-green leaves, bearing large double, loose clusters of fragrant flowers in hues of pink and white.

'**Madame Zoetmans**' Densely petalled, usually quartered flowers with a central green button. 1.2 × 1m/4 × 3ft

DAMASK ROSES

Kazanlük in Bulgaria is renowned for its otto or attar of roses. It takes 4kg of blooms to produce 1gm of rose oil.

Damask roses make wonderful floriferous hedges as well as providing form to a planting of perennials. They may be trimmed to shape.

'**Léda**' (The Painted Damask) Reddish-brown buds opening to milky-white blooms suffused with blush-pink – unmistakably marked with carmine tones. Beautifully scented. 1 × 1m/3 × 3ft

◆ *'Léda' makes a good sturdy bush with very dark green leaves.*

DAMASK ROSES

'Gloire de Guilan' Highly fragrant fully double, flat quartered blooms. Light green foliage and numerous thorns. 1.2 × 1.2m/4 × 4ft

◆ *This sprawling rose is grown for producing attar of roses.*

'Ispahan' ('Pompon des Princes') Pretty clusters on a fine bushy shrub. Creates a long and brilliant display. 1.5 × 1.2m/5 × 4ft

'Madame Hardy' blushed flesh-pink at first – opening to pure white. 1.5 × 1.5m/5 × 5ft

◆ *The cupped flowers reflex to reveal a green button eye.*

'Kazanlük' ('Trigintipetala') Grown for attar of roses and potpourri. Pale apple-green foliage, very fragrant flowers. 2 × 2m/6 × 6ft

'Celsiana' Pretty clusters of large semi-double pinky-white flowers. Very fragrant. 1.5 × 1.2m/5 × 4ft

'La Ville de Bruxelles' Fine luxuriant light green foliage and strong upright growth. Strong fragrance. 1.5 × 1m/5 × 3ft

'York and Lancaster' (*Rosa damascena versicolor*) Loosely formed semi-double flowers amid downy grey-green leaves. 2 × 2m/6 × 6ft

THE WHITE ROSES OF HISTORICAL IMPORTANCE, dating back to the Middle Ages. Handsome grey-green foliage, stems and hips. Tolerance of semi-shade and poor soil divulge the Dog rose as one parent; and the sweetly scented, tightly packed, very double blooms, in shades of pale pink and white are characteristic of *Rosa damascena*, the other. Remarkably versatile, as trained or specimen shrubs.

'Königin von Dänemark' ('Queen of Denmark') Carmine tinted buds opening to large, fragrant, distinctly quartered, pale-pink flowers with button centre. Dark blue-green foliage. 1.5 × 1.2m/5 × 4ft

'Alba semi-plena' Cluster of semi-double milky-white blooms with prominent golden stamens. Effective grey-green foliage. Round red hips in autumn. Very fragrant. 2 × 1.5m/6 × 5ft

'Great Maiden's Blush' ('Cuisse de Nymphe') Pale blush-pink, semi-double flowers with muddled centres, amid ample lush grey-green foliage. Strong sweet fragrance. 1.5 × 1.2m/5 × 4ft

Thorough soil preparation prior to planting is essential for establishing a good root system of any rose – even if it is 'tolerant of poor soil'.

Albas tolerate semi-shade; as in woodland plantings, where some varieties may be trained to climb into trees. No rose thrives in dense shade.

31

ALBA
ROSES

'Alba Maxima' Fully double slightly blushed flowers with muddled centres. Very fragrant. 2 × 1.5m/6 × 5ft

◆ *Also known as 'The Jacobite Rose' or 'White Rose of York'.*

'Félicité Parmentier' Unusually short for an Alba. Fresh-pink quartered blooms with button eye. 1.2 × 1.2m/4 × 4ft

'Celestial' ('Céleste') Rosy-pink buds opening to clear pale pink, semi-double flowers. Very scented. 2 × 1.5m/6 × 5ft

◆ *Perfectly scrolled buds make this a good cutting rose.*

'Madame Legras de St. Germain' Deliciously scented, slightly cupped, well filled blooms of glistening ivory-white flushed yellow. Graceful arching growth which may be trained to climb. 2 × 1.2m/6 × 4ft

ALSO KNOWN AS 'CABBAGE ROSES', as well as the 'Hundred-Leaved rose', hence the name Centifolia. Centifolias are notable for their distinctive flowers and foliage which scale precisely in accordance with the size of the shrub, ranging from large to miniature. The blooms are large, heavy and globular, reflexing to reveal the famous quartered centre and green button eye.

Rosa centifolia ('The Provence Rose', 'The Cabbage Rose') Large, clear-pink flowers. 2 × 1.5m/6 × 5ft

'Pompon de Bourgogne' ('Parvifolia', 'Burgundy Rose') A miniature bushy shrub bearing rosette-type flowers. 1m × 60cm/3 × 2ft

'Chapeau de Napoléon' ('Cristata', 'Napoleon's Hat', 'Crested Moss') Beautiful blooms with winged calyx. 1.5 × 1.2m/5 × 4ft

'Fantin Latour' Fragrant cupped flowers, packed with blush-pink petals deepening towards the centre – classically quartered with button eye. Later the outer petals reflex. 2 × 1.5m/6 × 5ft

'De Meaux' A short bushy shrub of fastigiate habit, bearing miniature Centifolia-type, pale grey-green foliage and tiny pink flat rosette-shaped flowers. 1 × 1m/3 × 3ft

◆ *This rose is very prone to black spot.*

CENTIFOLIA ROSES

The tall varieties are open and lax requiring some support while the miniatures are bushy and compact enough to be grown in a pot.

After flowering reduce long canes by one third or more. All dead and twiggy wood should be removed. Trim miniature varieties hard.

Rosa centifolia, also known as 'The Provence Rose' – its superb flower forms are often depicted in paintings, thus the name 'Rose des Peintres'.

'Petite de Hollande'
('Pompon des Dames')
Beautiful, fragrant flowers.
1.2 × 1m/4 × 3ft

◆ *'Petite de Hollande' makes a compact leafy shrub.*

Above from left to right: 'Ombrée Parfaite', 'Juno', 'Robert le Diable', 'Chapeau de Napoléon', 'Fantin Latour'. Huge heavy globular opulent blooms containing one hundred petals.

'Spong' Miniature, cupped, rich-pink flowers – slightly larger than 'Rose de Meaux', opening flat on a compact upright shrub with rounded grey-green leaves. 1.2 × 1m/4 × 3ft

MOSS ROSES

ROSA CENTIFOLIA MUSCOSA. Developed from a mossy mutation or sport of *Rosa centifolia*. Moss roses added novelty to rose breeding, concentrating innovations towards richly colourful, luxuriantly textured, resin-scented, mossy growths round the calyxes and stems. Not to the detriment of the blooms – which with their rich tones and deep fragrance took on a new exotic appearance! Often repeat-flowering.

The buds of Moss roses are covered in numerous variants of fascinating resinous moss. They open slowly, revealing richly colourful, deeply fragrant blooms.

'Madame Delaroche-Lambert' Brownish-green mossy buds opening to fragrant, crimson-purple, flattish flowers with rolled outer petals and muddled centres. Dark healthy foliage. Repeats well. 1.2 × 1.2m/4 × 4ft

'Gloire des Mousseux' ('Madame Alboni') Enormous full-petalled blooms of clear bright pink. 1.2 × 1m/4 × 3ft

◆ *Buds are lightly mossed amid plentiful light green foliage.*

'Blanche Moreau' A vigorous, slender, somewhat lax shrub.. Often recurrent. 2 × 1.2m/6 × 4ft

'Capitaine John Ingram' Tightly packed, slightly mossy buds opening to flat, compact, pompon-shaped blooms. 1.2 × 1m/4 × 3ft

MOSS ROSES

'Proliferation' is when the vegetative part of a bud develops from inside-out, resulting in severe malformation. It can be caused by extreme temperature fluctuations.

Don't fork round the roots of a rose – carefully apply herbicide to rid perennial weeds and maintain a generous mulch.

'Alfred de Dalmas' ('Mousseline') Sweetly scented creamy-white tinged pink, loosely formed blooms. A compact twiggy bush. 1.2 × 1.2m/4 × 4ft

◆ *'Alfred de Dalmas' flowers freely from midsummer to autumn.*

'Général Kléber' Soft bright green mossy buds opening to informal, double shining blooms, very fragrant, in soft pure pink, amid ample bright fresh foliage. 1.2 × 1.2m/4 × 4ft

'Henri Martin' Makes a tall graceful shrub. Clusters of small, tightly packed, clear-crimson flowers. Fairly fragrant. 1.5 × 1.2m/5 × 4ft

'Louis Gimard' Dark, mossy, densely packed buds opening to large flat blooms with muddled centres. Very fragrant. 1.5 × 1m/5 × 3ft

'William Lobb' ('Old Velvet Moss') Large clusters of blooms which fade to lavender-grey tinted with white. 2.4 × 1.5m/8 × 5ft

3. OLD SHRUB ROSES (REPEAT FLOWERING)

Cherished in small gardens today for their distinction and flexibility.

CHINA ROSES

China roses are surprisingly tough and vigorous, flowering continuously all summer. Many are capable of climbing to a considerable height.

'Old Blush China' is often seen blooming on Christmas day. Hellebores are the other 'Christmas roses'.

VIGOROUS, BUSHY, SOMEWHAT TWIGGY SHRUBS, which will flower continuously all summer, and often longer when positioned in a sheltered spot. Despite the fragile appearance of the exquisite flowers (in a mouth-watering range of hues) and dainty foliage, the shrubs are extremely hardy and very versatile. They may be pruned hard, trained against a wall or allowed to scrabble randomly.

'Viridiflora' ('The Green Rose') The petals and sepals apparently merge – green tinged with brown! A vigorous upright free-flowering shrub popular for flower arrangements. Odd peppery fragrance. $1 \times 1m/3 \times 3ft$

'Old Blush China' ('Parson's Pink China', 'The Monthly Rose') Clusters of delicate lilac-pink sweetly scented flowers on a dainty twiggy shrub. $1.2 \times 1m/ 4 \times 3ft$

'Irene Watts' Salmony-pink pointed buds open to full, flat, loosely double flowers. Very free-flowering. Bushy dark green purple-tinted foliage. $60 \times 60cm/2 \times 2ft$

'Hermosa' Small cupped lilac-pink blooms produced continuously throughout the season. 1 × 1m/3 × 3ft

'Mutabilis' ('Tipo Ideale', *Rosa turkestana*) Single papery flowers borne on delicate airy panicles. 1.2 × 1m/4 × 3ft

'Bloomfield Abundance' Miniature blooms borne at the tips of huge airy panicles. Upright wiry growth. 2 × 1.2m/6 × 4ft

'Sophie's Perpetual' Sprays of shapely, double, silvery-pink globe-shaped blooms. Sweetly scented. 2 × 1.2m/6 × 4ft

◆ *A twiggy shrub with healthy dark green foliage.*

Autumn Damask Roses

The other name for these roses is Portland roses.

Remarkable for their ability to flower intermittently from midsummer until autumn, greatly extending the rose season. Shorter and more compact than the Damasks; the stronger tones, very double flowers and rich fragrance are among the main virtues of these very useful shrubs in today's gardens. They were acclaimed after 1800 but were superseded in cultivation and popularity by the Hybrid Perpetuals.

'Portland Rose' Prolific bright crimson, semi-double, fragrant blooms, displaying bright golden stamens. Vigorous and sturdy growth with excellent mid-green foliage. 60 × 60cm/2 × 2ft

◆ *If dead blooms are removed, the 'Portland Rose' will remain in flower from midsummer until autumn.*

'Rose du Roi' (*Rosa paestana*, 'Scarlet Four Seasons') Parent of the Hybrid perpetuals. Large, fragrant, very double bright crimson-red flowers on a sturdy vigorous shrub. 1 × 1m/3 × 3ft

'Rose de Rescht' Small, neat, extremely fragrant, glowing-crimson lightening to magenta, pompon-shaped flowers. Short bushy shrub with dark purplish-green foliage. 1 × 1m/3 × 3ft

◆ *The beautiful quartering of these blooms which are borne from midsummer until autumn make this rose well worth growing.*

'Comte de Chambord' Large globular buds opening to very fragrant full flat quartered lilac-pink blooms. Forms a nice upright shrub if kept pruned. 1.2m × 1m/4 × 3ft

'Jacques Cartier' A vigorous yet short and compact bush. Delicious fragrance. 1.2 × 1m/4 × 3ft

◆ *'Jacques Cartier' is a very reliable repeat flowerer.*

'Quatre Saisons' (*Rosa damascena bifera*, 'The Rose of Four Seasons') Parent of the Bourbon roses. 1.5 × 1.5m/5 × 5ft

Shorter and more compact than the Damasks, Damask Perpetuals make excellent hedges; some varieties grow well in a pot.

If roses show signs of potassium deficiency, banana skins may be your answer! Strewn beneath the mulch, roses rapidly absorb this valuable source of potassium.

Bourbon Roses

Bourbons require good pruning to succeed. In winter reduce long canes by one third, and cut side-shoots back to three eyes ('spur pruning').

'Boule de Neige' Clusters of sweetly scented, quartered blooms which reflex into a ball.
1.2 × 1m/4 × 3ft

'Souvenir de la Malmaison' Soft flesh-pink cups opening to huge, regularly quartered, sweetly fragrant blooms. 1 × 1m/3 × 3ft

'Souvenir de Saint Anne's' Very fragrant flowers in perfect formation amid good foliage.
2 × 1.5m/6 × 5ft

'Madame Isaac Pereire' Enormous, cupped and quartered blooms amid abundant, dark foliage. 2 × 1.5m/ 6 × 5ft

◆ *This rose may be trained to climb.*

'Louise Odier' Perfectly assembled cup-shaped blooms. Very perpetual and fragrant. 1.5 × 1.2m/5 × 4ft

'Madame Pierre Oger' A short, bushy sport of 'Reine Victoria'. Very pale blooms intensify in sunny weather.
1.2 × 1.2m/4 × 4ft

IN 1817 A CHANCE SEEDLING WAS DISCOVERED on the Isle de Bourbon east of Madagascar – probably a cross between the two cultivars 'Quatre Saisons' and 'Old Blush China', commonly used as hedging. By intercrossing it with Gallicas and Damasks the Bourbons developed. The flowers are round and full-petalled, richly fragrant in bold tones and stripes and appear intermittently all summer, some of their finest blooms borne in late summer. Dead-head and feed, following the first burst of bloom.

BOURBON ROSES

'Reine Victoria' A tall slender shrub bearing soft, cupped blooms. Very fragrant and perpetual. 2 × 1m/6 × 3ft

'Honorine de Brabant' Very vigorous with handsome light green foliage. 2 × 1.5m/6 × 5ft

'Variegata di Bologna' Strong arching growth bearing spectacular, fragrant, fully cupped, double flowers. 1.5 × 1.2m/5 × 4ft

◆ *'Variegata di Bologna' is also a strong climber.*

HYBRID PERPETUAL ROSES

DESCENDANTS OF AUTUMN DAMASKS, BOURBONS AND CHINAS, predecessors of Hybrid Teas. Popular with Victorians who enjoyed them pegged down in beds, trained up pillars, floated in water and worn in their hair! Ranging from short bushes to tall lax shrubs, the flowers are full, richly perfumed in gorgeous hues of maroon, purple, crimson and violet, in successive crops throughout the summer.

'Baron Girod de L'Ain'
Bright crimson-red flowers with marked white edging to each petal. The flower-form is cupped in the centre, reflexed at the edges. 1.5 × 1.2m/5 × 4ft

'Frau Karl Druschki'
('Snow Queen') Pink-tinted buds opening to large pure-white flowers with notable high lemon-tinted centres. Light green foliage. Vigorous erect growth. 1.5 × 1m/5 × 3ft

'Général Jacqueminot' A vigorous shrub with Damask fragrance and abundant fresh-green foliage. 1.5 × 1.2m/5 × 4ft

'Hugh Dickson' Perfumed and free-flowering, it produces such long shoots it could almost be treated as a climber. 2.4 × 1.5m/8 × 5ft

'Reine des Violettes'
Grape-purple fading to warm parma-violet. Vigorous growth, few thorns. 1.5 × 1m/5 × 3ft

'Ulrich Brunner Fils'
Vigorous upright habit with luxuriant foliage. Deeply fragrant. 2.2 × 1.2m/7 × 4ft

Right: **'Baroness Rothschild'** at the centre of a selection of rich Hybrid Perpetuals, including **'Souvenir du Docteur Jamain'** (top left), **'Gloire de Ducher'** (top right), **'Ferdinand Pichard'** (bottom right) and **'Roger Lambelin'** (bottom left). Planting Hybrid Perpetuals in a border is a real opportunity for the artist's palette, in gorgeous hues of maroon, crimson and pink which co-ordinate on a par with asters.

4. MODERN SHRUB ROSES

*Relatively recent introductions – an
outstandingly useful collection of shrubs
which range from the giant and arching
to the dwarf and cushion-like.*

Hybrid Species Roses

'Anna Zinkeisen' Clusters of fragrant, fully double reflexing flowers. Prolific light-green glossy foliage. 1.2 × 1.2m/4 × 4ft

'Cerise Bouquet' Medium-sized, cerise-pink flowers, borne in sprays along arching stems. 2.7 × 2.7m/ 9 × 9ft

'Fritz Nobis' A very vigorous shrub with glossy dark green foliage. Summer flowering. Good hips. 1.5 × 1.2m/5 × 4ft

'Frühlingsgold' Masses of large, semi-double, pale-yellow flowers, deepening towards a showy golden boss, smother a luxuriantly foliated shrub. Very fragrant. 2.2 × 2m/7 × 6ft

'Gipsy Boy' ('Zigeunerknabe') Tolerates poor soil and part shade. Summer flowering. 1.5 × 1.2m/5 × 4ft

'Maigold' Vigorous prickly arching growth with bright glossy foliage. Good as a climber. 1.5 × 2.4m/5 × 8ft

'Marguerite Hilling' Warm rich-pink flowers contrast nicely with dark chocolate stems. 2.4 × 2.2m/8 × 7ft

'Frühlingsmorgen' A single, free-flowering rose of more compact growth than 'Frühlingsgold'. 2 × 1.5m/6 × 5ft

'Nevada' Fragrant flowers in profusion along arching stems. 2.4 × 2.2m/8 × 7ft

'Robbie Burns' Single, cupped, delicately fragrant flowers. Round black hips follow. 1.5 × 1.5m/5 × 5ft

'Scharlachglut' ('Scarlet Fire') Large, single flowers. Deep-red stems, arching growth. Large bottle-shaped hips. 2.2 × 2m/7 × 6ft

THESE ARE THE GIANTS OF MODERN SHRUB ROSES, very closely related to the Species roses. The flowers, reminiscent of the Dog roses, are brighter, larger and more double, giving a magnificent display in early summer often repeating in late summer. The shrubs are tough and are suitable as specimens, planted singly or in groups; as hedging and as screening.

HYBRID SPECIES ROSES

'Constance Spry' Large double, clear luminous-pink, globular blooms in profusion on a spectacular lax-growing shrub. Requires some support. Summer flowering. 2.4 × 2m/8 × 6ft

◆ *'Constance Spry' is a spectacular sight in midsummer trained as a climber, over a wall, fence or trellis.*

Dwarf Polyantha Roses

The other name for these roses is Poly-pom roses.

LOW-GROWING BUSHES UNRIVALLED FOR USEFULNESS, VIGOUR AND HEALTH, flowering continuously from midsummer until autumn. Clusters of exquisite fragrant flowers in shades of pink, lemon and white, mostly in small pompons or rosettes. Ideally suited for mixed borders, planted in groups amongst perennials and shrubs, and for carpeting beneath standard roses. Also suitable for pots.

'Francine Austin' Low arching growth with twiggy stems bearing dainty sprays of small, glistening-white pompons. 1 × 1.2m/3 × 4ft

◆ *This is a healthy and continuous bloomer.*

'Nathalie Nypels' Prolific, semi-double, bright pinky-white flowers with lemony stamens, on a vigorous but low, spreading bush. Healthy dark foliage. Very fragrant. 1 × 1m/3 × 3ft

'Yvonne Rabier' Clusters of small, double, pure-white flowers against dark, glossy, healthy foliage. 1.2 × 1m/ 4 × 3ft

'The Fairy' Massive sprays of perfectly formed small pale-pink rosettes. Delicate fragrance.
60cm × 1m/2 × 3ft

◆ *This rose makes a short, dense, spreading bush.*

DWARF POLYANTHA ROSES

Dwarf Polyantha or Poly-pom roses, sadly, have little fragrance, but grouped or mass-planted, their effect is unsurpassed for continuity of flower.

'Little White Pet' Perpetual flowering, panicles of small, white, double rosettes, pink in bud, amid dark foliage.
60 × 60cm/2 × 2ft

◆ *This rose is a dwarf sport of 'Félicité et Perpétue'.*

'Cécile Brunner' ('The Sweetheart Rose') Miniature shell-pink Hybrid Tea shaped blooms. Sweet scent. 1m × 60cm/3 × 2ft

'Perle d'Or' ('Yellow Cécile Brunner') Small, softly fragrant flowers on a short twiggy bush. 1m × 60cm/ 3 × 2ft

'Ballerina' Flowers borne in large, prolific corymbs, like those of a hydrangea.
1.2 × 1m/4 × 3ft

◆ *'Ballerina' makes a good miniature or half-standard rose for a pot.*

53

HYBRID MUSK ROSES

ROSA MOSCHATA HYBRIDS. Deliciously fragrant flowers in compatible shades of cream, pink, yellow and scarlet, in small clusters at midsummer, but producing magnificent, long panicles throughout late summer and autumn. Dark reddish-brown young stems and handsome foliage. Equally at home in a bed of their own, mixed border, as a hedge or trained over a trellis or fence.

'Buff Beauty' Large trusses of fully double, warm apricot blooms. 1.5 × 1.5m/5 × 5ft

♦ *'Buff Beauty' may be trained to climb.*

'Sally Holmes' Single flowers, borne in enormous corymbs. Vigorous erect habit. Large healthy foliage. 1.5 × 1.2m/5 × 4ft

'Moonlight' Enormous trusses of white flowers against dark foliage. Musk-rose fragrance. 1.5 × 1.2m/ 5 × 4ft

'Prosperity' Clusters of pinky-tinged buds opening to deliciously scented, ivory-white flowers tinted yellow at the centre. May be trained to climb. 1.5 × 1.2m/5 × 4ft

'Felicia' Large trusses bearing warm-pink buds tinted with apricot opening to silvery-pink semi-double flowers. Vigorous upright growth. Dark glossy foliage. 1.5 × 1.5m/5 × 5ft

'Penelope' Salmony-orange buds opening to semi-double blooms of creamy-pink, turning to white. Rich musk fragrance. 2 × 1.2m/6 × 4ft

◆ *'Penelope' produces beautiful cool-green, bloom-covered hips.*

A small garden of hybrid musks with peonies and other herbaceous planting.

'Cornelia' Large sprays bearing rich copper-tinted buds opening to small rosettes of salmon-pink turning to creamy-pink. May be trained to climb. 1.5 × 1.5m/5 × 5ft

◆ *It pays to remove the unsightly dead-heads of 'Cornelia'.*

ENGLISH ROSES

RELATIVELY RECENT INTRODUCTIONS with the unique charm reminiscent of Old roses having typical rosette or full-cupped, globular flowers and powerful individual fragrance. This is combined with repeat-flowering and the more compact habit of Modern Bush roses. The characterful flowers predominate over the non-distinctive but good, bushy habit, enlivening the limited range of cream, yellow, apricot and red hues.

'Perdita' Perfectly quartered flowers in deep cups of delicate creamy-apricot blushed with pink. Deep-green disease resistant foliage. Charming slightly lax habit. 1 × 1m/3 × 3ft

'Charles Austin' Large cupped full-petalled blooms with rich fruity fragrance. Vigorous upright growth which is excellent for cutting. 1.5 × 1.2m/5 × 4ft

'Graham Thomas' Fully double, softly cupped blooms, light green healthy foliage. 1.2 × 1.2m/4 × 4ft

'The Pilgrim' Soft yellow rosettes on a very robust free-flowering bush with shiny green leaves. 1.1 × 1m/3½ × 3ft

'Symphony' Sweetly fragrant blooms amid plentiful medium-green foliage. Short bushy habit. 1 × 1m/3 × 3ft

'Sweet Juliet' Shallow cupped and quartered flowers. Strong leafy upright growth. Very fragrant. 1.2 × 1m/4 × 3ft

'Cymbeline' Cool grey-blush flowers with a powerful myrrh fragrance on strong arching growth. 1.2 × 1.5m/4 × 5ft

'Lucetta' Strong arching growth bearing healthy dark foliage and semi-double flowers. 1.2 × 1.2m/4 × 4ft

'Charles Rennie Mackintosh' Tough, vigorous and bushy with fragrant flowers.
1m × 75cm/3 × 2½ft

'Sharifa Asma' Cupped at first, reflexing into deeply fragrant rosettes. Short, upright growth.
1m × 60cm/3 × 2ft

'Mary Rose' A good disease-resistant shrub with bright loosely formed flowers, only slighted scented. 1.2 × 1.2m/4 × 4ft

ENGLISH ROSES

The tendency to arch to the ground under the weight of the blooms is overcome by reducing canes by one half or more in winter.

'Heritage' Vigorous bushy habit bearing huge round, cupped blooms. Marvellous strong fragrance.
1.2 × 1.2m/4 × 4ft

'Prospero' A perfect rosette of rich deep crimson turning to purple. Low spreading shrub.
60cm × 1m/2 × 3ft

'Chianti' Gallica-type rosettes. Richly perfumed. Summer flowering.
1.5 × 1.5m/5 × 5ft

'L.D. Braithwaite' Blooms freely produced over a long period of time. Lovely 'Old rose' fragrance. Unaffected by rain. 1.2 × 1.2m/4 × 4ft

'Gertrude Jekyll' Pretty buds opening to large fragrant blooms.
1.2 × 1m/4 × 3ft

◆ *Upright, robust and very healthy foliage.*

GROUND-COVER ROSES

THE VICTORIANS USED ROSES AS BEDDING. Modern landscapers have given breeders a similar specification but emphasize low-maintenance as the priority. Ground-cover roses range from huge trailing sprawlers which can smother and transform dull banks, to low-growing, compact shrubs, forming mounds of brightness and texture; and miniature carpeters which hug the sides of pots!

'Raubritter' Low trailing mounds bearing clusters of semi-double very cupped lilac-pink flowers in profusion. Attractive greyish foliage. Slight fragrance. Summer flowering. 1 × 1.5m/3 × 5ft

'Paulii' Vigorous thorny shoots form a dense, low, spreading mound. Large single pure-white papery flowers with crinkled petals, scented of cloves. Summer flowering. 1 × 2.7m/3 × 9ft

'Red Max Graf' Low and spreading, bushy shrub. Bright coppery-green, glossy foliage. Flowers midsummer onwards. 60cm × 1.5m/2 × 5ft

'Red Blanket' Scarlet-red flowers all summer with excellent shiny disease-resistant foliage. 1.2 × 1.5m/4 × 5ft

'Pink Bells' Rich-pink pompons borne in sprays amid small dark glossy healthy foliage. Forms a cushion. Flowers midsummer onwards. 60cm × 1.2m/2 × 4ft

'Rosy Cushion' Very similar in habit to 'Red Blanket'. Flowers continuously all summer. 1.2 × 1.5m/4 × 5ft

Descending the steps: **'Red Max Graf'**, *Verbascum chaixii* 'Album', 'Pink Bells', *Eremurus robustus* 'Alba', **'Raubritter'**, **'Rosy Cushion', 'Snow Carpet'**, *Bergenia* 'Admiral' form carpets, cascades and cushions, smothering the side of the steps and climbing into a steep bank emphasized by occasional spiky perennials.

5. CLIMBING ROSES

Climbing roses all have one thing in common – they climb! But their flower-shapes, scent, climbing habit and vigorousness are largely in accordance with their parentage.

CLIMBING NOISETTE ROSES

'Alister Stella Grey' ('Golden Rambler') Small clusters – increasing as summer goes on – of loosely formed, fragrant yellow flowers with dark centres. Also good as a shrub. 5 × 3m/16 × 10ft

'Gloire de Dijon' ('The Old Glory Rose') Very large, extremely fragrant, full-cupped and quartered flowers of buffy pinky-apricot tones. Vigorous leafy growth. Tolerates part shade. 3.5 × 2.4m/12 × 8ft

'Madame Alfred Carrière' Prolific clusters of large, informally double, fragrant, white tinged with pink blooms. Vigorous, fairly thorn-free, light green foliage. Tolerates partial shade. 3.5 × 3m/12 × 10ft

'Goldfinch' Large tightly-packed clusters of small semi-double flowers – golden-yellow on opening turning to cream with dark orange stamens. Summer flowering. 3 × 2m/10 × 6ft

'Meg' Beautiful, large, open semi-double flowers. 3.5 × 2m/12 × 6ft

◆ *Meg's dark glossy foliage is a good setting for the delicate blooms.*

'Cécile Brunner' A vigorous climber with tiny Hybrid Tea-shaped blooms. 5 × 3m/16 × 10ft

BRED FROM AN ORIGINAL CROSS between 'Parson's Pink China' and *Rosa moschata*, which was brought to France from America in the 1800s: prolific clusters of highly fragrant rosette-type flowers in delicate shades of pink, yellow and white.

CLIMBING NOISETTE ROSES

'Blush Noisette' The original Noisette rose. Clusters of medium-sized prettily cupped, pinky-white flowers. Sweetly scented of cloves. Very continuous. Also good as a shrub. 2.2 × 1.2m/7 × 4ft

◆ *Climbing Noisettes flower mostly from summer until autumn, thriving on a sunny wall, trellis, arch or pergola – protected from frost and cold winds.*

LARGE-FLOWERED CLIMBING ROSES

D<small>ERIVATIVES OF MANY FAVOURITES IN THE BOOK</small> – <small>WHICH CAN</small> <small>CLIMB.</small> They all bear large fragrant, conspicuous flowers in an exciting range of shapes, formations and colours. An eye-catching spectacle trained up a wall, pillar, fence or trellis; some varieties tolerant of shady aspects; most performing repeat displays throughout summer and often into autumn. Large-flowered climbing roses are often climbing versions or 'sports' of Bush roses. Distinguishable from other climbing roses by their large, bright blooms.

'Dortmund' Clusters of single blooms – followed by hips. 2.4 × 2m/8 × 6ft

◆ *'Dortmund' is good as a hedge.*

'Madame Grégoire Staechelin' ('Spanish Beauty') Summer flowering. 5 × 3m/16 × 10ft

'Zéphirine Drouhin' (Bourbon) Flowers borne on thornless stems. Tolerates part shade. 3 × 2m/10 × 6ft

'Blairii Number Two' (Bourbon) Large, fragrant, globular very double blooms. 3.5 × 2m/12 × 6ft

'Aloha' Fully petalled blooms on strong upright growth with dark leathery foliage. Very fragrant. 3 × 1.5m/10 × 5ft

'Lady Hillingdon'
(Climbing Tea) Large, rich apricot-yellow blooms which hang their heads.
3.5 × 2.4m/12 × 8ft

'Alchemist' Large full rosette-shaped flowers. Summer flowering. 3.5 × 2.4m/12 × 8ft

'Mermaid' Large, single, sulphur-yellow flowers with deep amber stamens. Vigorous growth. 8 × 3.5m/26 × 12ft

◆ *'Mermaid' requires a high wall sheltered from cold winds.*

'Compassion' Typical Hybrid Tea-shaped flowers. Vigorous upright growth bearing dark stems and dark glossy healthy foliage. 3 × 2m/10 × 6ft

'Leverkusen' A vigorous shrub or climber. Mid-green glossy, serrated foliage, with clusters of medium sized, loosely-double, lemon-yellow, sweetly fragrant flowers. 3 × 2m/10 × 6ft

'New Dawn' Fragrant flowers amid healthy glossy dark foliage. Tolerates part shade. 3.5 × 2.4m/12 × 8ft

'Souvenir de la Malmaison' (Bourbon). Flowers twice: in midsummer and late summer. 3.5 × 2.4m/12 × 8ft

'Sombreuil' (Tea Climber) Fully double flat, quartered blooms. Delicious Tea scent. Ample lush-green foliage. 2.4 × 1.5m/8 × 5ft

65

RAMBLER ROSES

EXTREMELY VIGOROUS CREEPING GROWTH, bearing huge trusses of small flowers in a prolific display during early to midsummer – filling the air with fragrance, sometimes repeating late summer. Unrivalled floriferous coverage for pillars, arches, pergolas, arbours and fences, intensified when combined with Noisettes, Large-flowered climbers and clematis. The most vigorous varieties may be trained up into trees.

When the main flush of (from left to right) **'Léontine Gervais'**, **'Félicité et Perpétue'**, **'Violette'** is over, the *Clematis* 'Jackmanii Superba' bridges the gap until **'Aimée Vibert'** and **'Cécile Brunner'** arrive for late summer.

'Albéric Barbier'
(Wichuraiana) Yellow buds opening to fully double creamy-white fragrant flowers with almost evergreen, ample glossy foliage. Repeats in late summer. 5 × 3m/16 × 10ft

Arches, pergolas and trellis
divide the space and create
rooms and walkways. They
quickly make a garden
three-dimensional and
interesting.

Don't cut back new growth
on Ramblers – they may
never have flowers! It is
these new growths which
bear the flowers the
following season.

'Bobbie James' (Multiflora)
Exceptionally large corymbs
bearing sweetly scented,
creamy-white, semi-double
flowers. Makes massive
growth with its abundant
light green foliage.
10 × 7m/33 × 23ft

'Francis E. Lester'
(Moschata hybrid) Huge
fragrant clusters of neat
single flowers – pink in bud,
opening to pinky-white,
followed by small orange-
red hips. 5 × 3m/16 × 10ft

'Paul's Himalayan Musk'
(Moschata hybrid) Vigorous
graceful growth bearing
long trailing shoots and
dainty hanging sprays of
small double blush-pink
rosettes. Very fragrant.
10 × 7m/33 × 23ft

6. MODERN BUSH ROSES

Bush roses, compared to the intoxicating subtleties of Shrub roses, bring to the garden a palette of sharpened brightness. For this they should be exploited.

HYBRID TEA ROSES

THE MOST POPULAR GARDEN ROSES OF THIS CENTURY. They followed after the Hybrid Perpetuals. Strong stems bearing large, solitary, upheld flowers, they demonstrate the exquisite variation in detail sought after by breeders in pursuit of the perfect bloom, encouraged by fashion and competition. Their rich satin-textured petals exemplify the multitude of hues. Suitable as bedding or border plants or for massed display.

'Simba' Exceptionally high-centred with very long petals – beautifully shaped in pure bright yellow. They appear dazzling against the abundant mid-green foliage.
75 × 75cm/2½ × 2½ft

'Just Joey' Fragrant blooms become extremely large in warm weather.
75 × 60cm/2½ × 2ft

'Ingrid Bergman' Large blooms borne on a strong upright free-flowering shrub. Good for cutting.
1m × 60cm/3 × 2ft

'Tequila Sunrise' Showy with a scarlet edging to its gold blooms. Glossy foliage.
75 × 75cm/2½ × 2½ft

'Doris Tysterman' Vigorous and upright in habit with bronze-green foliage. Slight fragrance.
1m × 75cm/3 × 2½ft

'Mrs Oakley Fisher' Graceful old single-flowered Hybrid Tea which is well scented. Bronze foliage.
1m × 1m/3 × 3ft

'Super Star' Flamboyant, for those who like brilliant colour. Fragrant. Branching growth. 1 × 1m/3 × 3ft

'Keepsake' Finely shaped glowing blooms, lightly scented. Upright and vigorous. Glossy leaves.
1 × 1m/3 × 3ft

'Alec's Red' Heavily scented and well formed blooms very freely produced. Dark glossy leaves. 1m × 75cm/3 × 2½ft

'Silver Jubilee' Elegant, finely formed flowers on a vigorous bush, well clothed with healthy foliage. 75 × 75cm/2½ × 2½ft

'Fragrant Cloud' Large perfumed flowers, very freely produced on a vigorous bush. 1 × 1m/3 × 3ft

'Royal William' Classic velvety blooms. Strong-necked, robust and healthy. 1 × 1m/3 × 3ft

◆ *One of the most fragrant of Modern Bush roses.*

FLORIBUNDA ROSES

Floribunda roses originated from a cross between a Hybrid Tea and a Polyantha rose in the 1920s. Their other name is Cluster-flowered roses.

THE FLOWERS OF FLORIBUNDAS ARE CARRIED IN CLUSTERS OR SPRAYS creating a vivid and often dramatic spectacle from early summer to autumn, particularly when planted in groups or in massed displays. Useful as border plants and as hedging. The smaller varieties may be grown in containers.

'Anne Harkness' Sprays of warm gold/apricot flowers. Healthy, could form a hedge. 1.2 × 1m/4 × 3ft

'Amber Queen' The rich amber is in harmony with the bronze-tinted leaves. 60 × 60cm/2 × 2ft

◆ *A very fragrant rose with spreading habit.*

'Mountbatten' Vigorous and shrubby with dark foliage and luminous double flowers. 1.2 × 1m/4 × 3ft

'City of Leeds' Reliable shrub with bronze-green foliage and freely produced clusters of blooms. 75 × 75cm/2½ × 2½ft

'Korresia' Very fragrant, long-lasting flowers on a compact bush. 75 × 75cm/2½ × 2½ft

'Matangi' One of the most vivid floribundas. Very flamboyant. Dark foliage. 75 × 75cm/2½ × 2½ft

'Sexy Rexy' Surprising name for a pretty double rose. Good bushy growth up to 1.2 × 1m/4 × 3ft

'Queen Elizabeth' The popular back-of-border or hedging rose. Strong and vigorous. 1.5 × 1m/5 × 3ft

'Escapade' Large single flowers like a wild rose, lilac to pink. Good mixer in a border. 1.2 × 1.2m/4 × 4ft

FLORIBUNDA ROSES

Liquid concentrated seaweed extract is excellent foliar feed. Add it to your fungicide and achieve two aims. Always spray when conditions are calm, preferably in the evening.

'Gruss an Aachen' Deep full cups in the Old rose style. Powerful fragrance. bushy upright growth. 60 × 60cm/2 × 2ft

'News' Large clusters of semi-double fullish blooms. Echoes its parent 'Tuscany Superb' (Gallica). 75 × 75cm/2½ × 2½ft

'Iceberg' The famous prolific white Floribunda, with pretty buds opening to wide double blossoms. 1.2 × 1.2m/4 × 4ft

◆ *'Iceberg' is a valuable bush rose for borders.*

Roses in unusual shades of copper, **'Edith Holden'** (in front), and pink with buff **'Iced Ginger'** (in the background), combine with perennials *Iris* 'Perryhill', the bright-scarlet spikes of *Penstemon barbatus* and ornamental grass *Ophiopogon planiscapus* 'Nigrescens'.

THE EARLY FLORIBUNDAS WERE IN PINKS AND REDS, then came the yellows. More recently the artist-breeder has dabbled with heavenly tones of apricot and copper and, on another note, revelled in ambiguous shades of lavender, mauve and brown! These innovations are curiosities on their own but can provide a source of inspiration for creating exciting planting schemes and flower arrangements.

FLORIBUNDA ROSES

'Lavender Pinocchio' A stunning little rose in both colour and form.
75 × 75cm/2½ × 2½ft

'Magenta' Clusters of 'Old Rose' rosettes in delicate shades of mauvish magenta-blue – the petals textured like porcelain. Fairly vigorous and fragrant.
1.5 × 1.2m/5 × 4ft

'Lilac Charm' An exquisite single flower in the palest lilac-mauve with prominent bushy red stamens borne on a compact bush with dark matt foliage.
60 × 60cm/2 × 2ft

'Brown Velvet' Russet-brown blooms borne freely amid bronze-green foliage.
75 × 60cm/2½ × 2ft

◆ *A good rose for flower arrangers.*

MINIATURE *and* PATIO ROSES

VERSATILITY IS AN INVALUABLE COMMODITY FOR ROSES in the modern small garden: be it patio, courtyard or balcony. The miniature, often rounded habit of these roses is ideally suited to forming neat, round cushions in paviour crevices and pots; also as low hedging and, where scale matters, in borders. The range of flower-shapes available in miniature form is extensive.

'The Valois Rose' (Patio) Double blooms, creamy yellow in bud deepening to carmine edges in maturity. 60cm/2ft

◆ *A vigorous, upright grower.*

'City Lights' (Patio) Classically shaped blooms on a vigorous bush to 60cm/2ft

'Perestroika' (Miniature) Little bright yellow blooms with reflexed petals cover bronze-green leaves. 45cm/1½ft

'Pretty Polly' (Miniature)
The bush has a rounded
habit, covered with
charming delicate blooms.
45cm/1½ft

'Gentle Touch' (Miniature)
Dainty flowers on a bushy
little shrub. 45cm/1½ft

MINIATURE *and* PATIO ROSES

Miniature and Patio roses
provide a long and dazzling
display of colour and
interest, requiring less
maintenance than, say,
bedding annuals.

Hanging baskets and pots
are both suitable for
growing Miniature and
Patio roses. Train a dense
creeper to shade the roots
from drying out.

'Sweet Dream' (Patio)
Upright growth, clustered
with very neat full-petalled
flowers with some scent.
45cm/1½ft

'Queen Mother' (Patio)
Rather like a miniature
Shrub rose – very strong
growing, good in a border
or pot. 75cm/2½ft

'Regensberg' (Patio) A
rounded bush smothered
with dramatic bright pink,
white-eyed flowers.
45cm/1½ft

'Top Marks' (Miniature)
Small brilliant orange-
vermillion flowers and
glossy foliage. 45cm/1½ft
but shown here as a
standard.

'Sweet Magic' (Miniature)
Small neat gold and orange
blooms mass a well-foliaged
little bush to 45cm/1½ft.

'Scarlet Patio' (Patio)
Cluster of intensely
coloured flowers against
deep green glossy leaves.
Compact. 45cm/1½ft

'Snow Sunblaze'
(Miniature) Small very
double buds open into
reflexed blooms on this
little bush. 30cm/1ft

INDEX OF ROSES